W9-AAT-684

HOORAY FOR NURSES!

by Elle Parkes

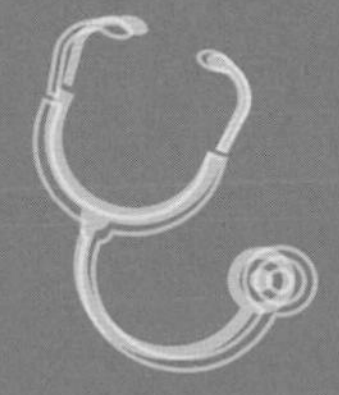

LERNER PUBLICATIONS ◆ MINNEAPOLIS

Note to Educators:

Throughout this book, you'll find critical thinking questions. These can be used to engage young readers in thinking critically about the topic and in using the text and photos to do so.

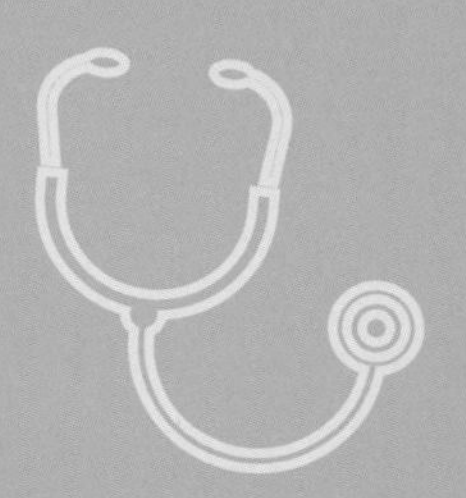

Lerner Publications Company
A division of Lerner Publishing Group, Inc.
241 First Avenue North
Minneapolis, MN 55401 USA

For reading levels and more information, look up this title at www.lernerbooks.com.

Library of Congress Cataloging-in-Publication Data

Names: Parkes, Elle.
Title: Hooray for nurses! / by Elle Parkes.
Description: Minneapolis : Lerner Publications, [2017] | Series: Bumba books—Hooray for community helpers! | Audience: Age 4–8. | Audience: K to grade 3. | Includes index.
Identifiers: LCCN 2016001283 (print) | LCCN 2016011118 (ebook) | ISBN 9781512414448 (lb : alk. paper) | ISBN 9781512414790 (pb : alk. paper) | ISBN 9781512414806 (eb pdf)
Subjects: LCSH: Nurses—Juvenile literature. | Nursing—Juvenile literature.
Classification: LCC RT61.5 .P37 2017 (print) | LCC RT61.5 (ebook) | DDC 610.73—dc23

LC record available at http://lccn.loc.gov/2016001283

Manufactured in the United States of America
1 – VP – 7/15/16

Table of Contents

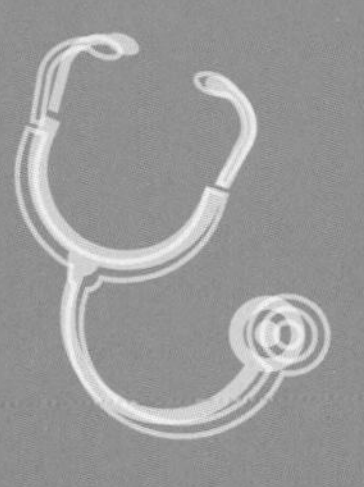

Nurses Keep Us Healthy

Nurses help keep people healthy.

They work with doctors.

Nurses work in hospitals.

They help patients.

Patients are sick or hurt people.

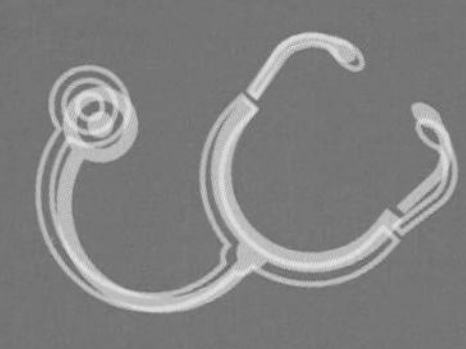

Some nurses care for new babies.

These nurses help new mothers too.

Why might new mothers need a nurse's help?

Nurses also work
in schools.
They take care
of sick students.

Where else do you think nurses can work?

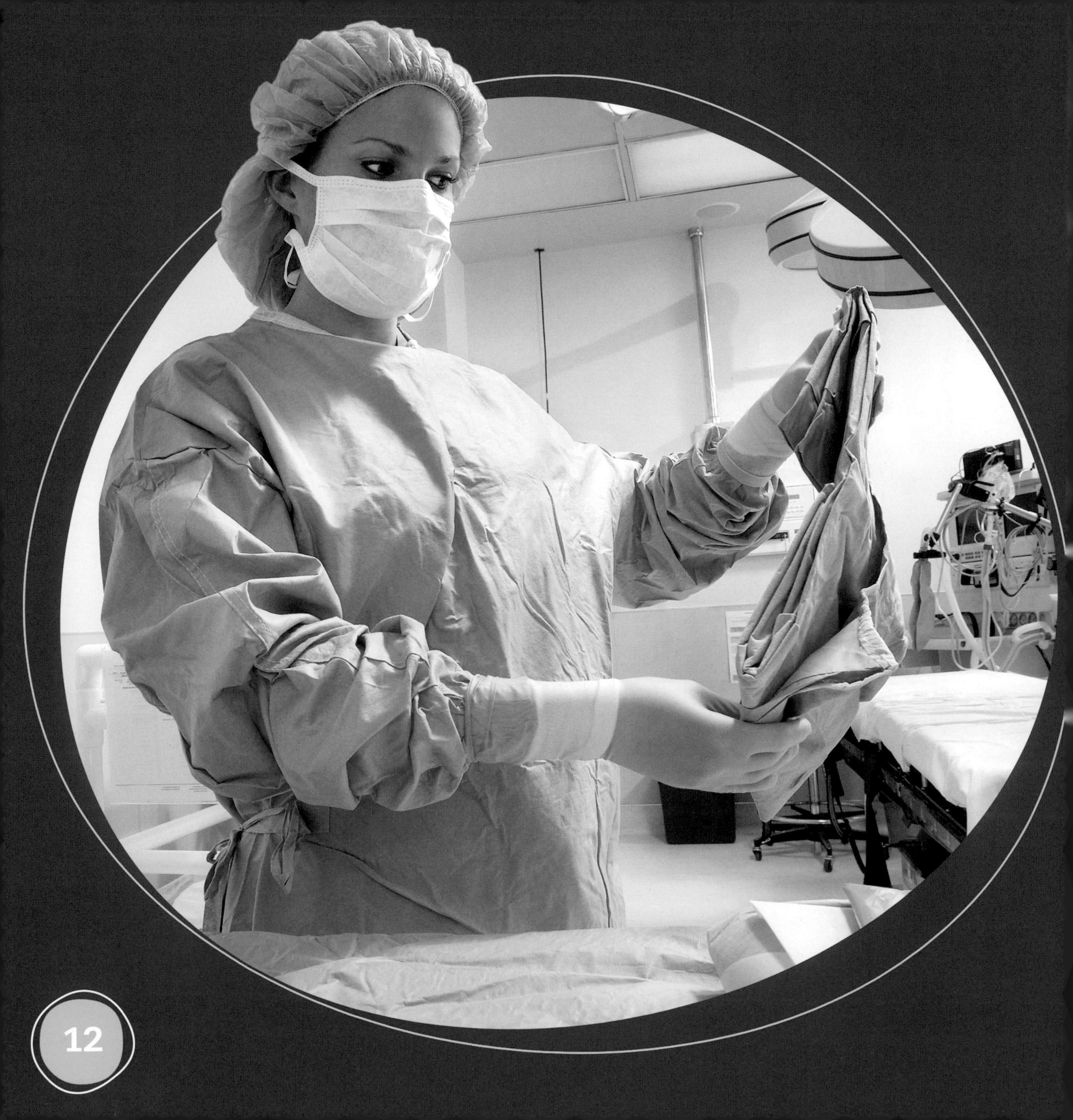

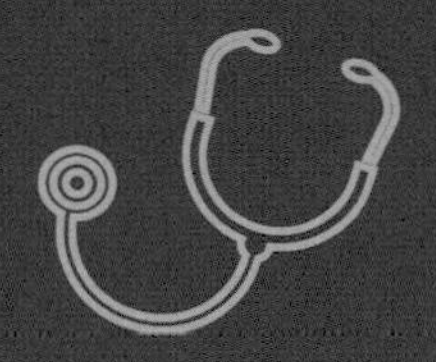

Nurses wear uniforms.

They are called scrubs.

Sometimes they wear gloves.

Uniforms keep nurses safe

from germs.

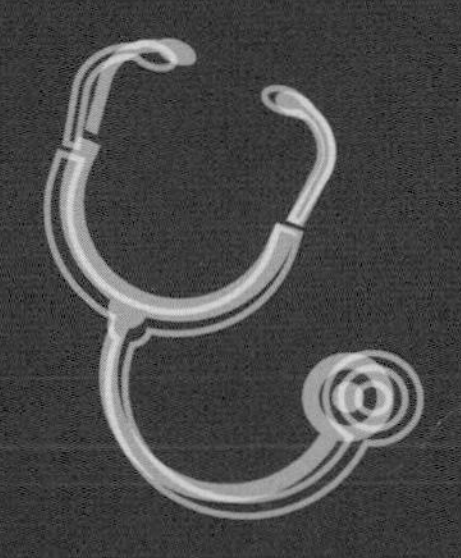

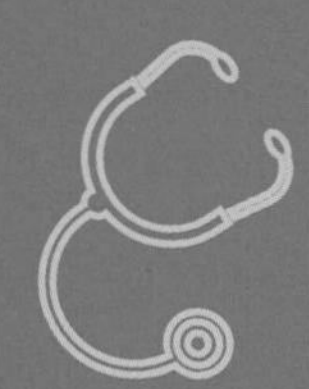

Nurses use special tools.

A scale checks weight.

A thermometer checks your temperature.

Why should nurses check your weight?

lbs 480 460 440 420 400 380 360 340 320 300 280 260 240 220 200
120
60 40 20 0

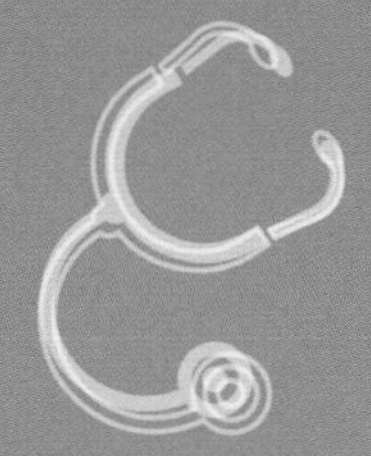

Nurses give people medicine.

Sometimes nurses give a pill.

Other times nurses give a shot.

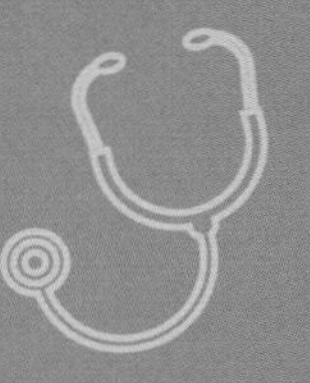

Nurses go to school

for many years.

Then they are ready

to help patients.

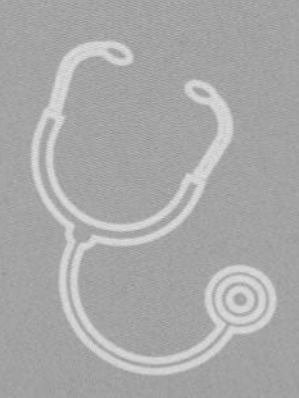

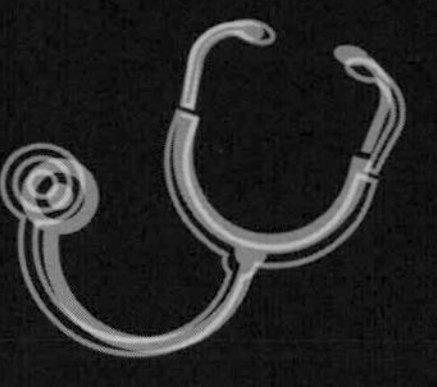

Nurses work long hours.

Caring for others is very important to them.

Nurse Tools

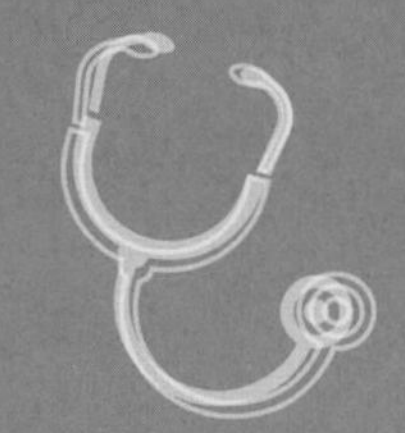

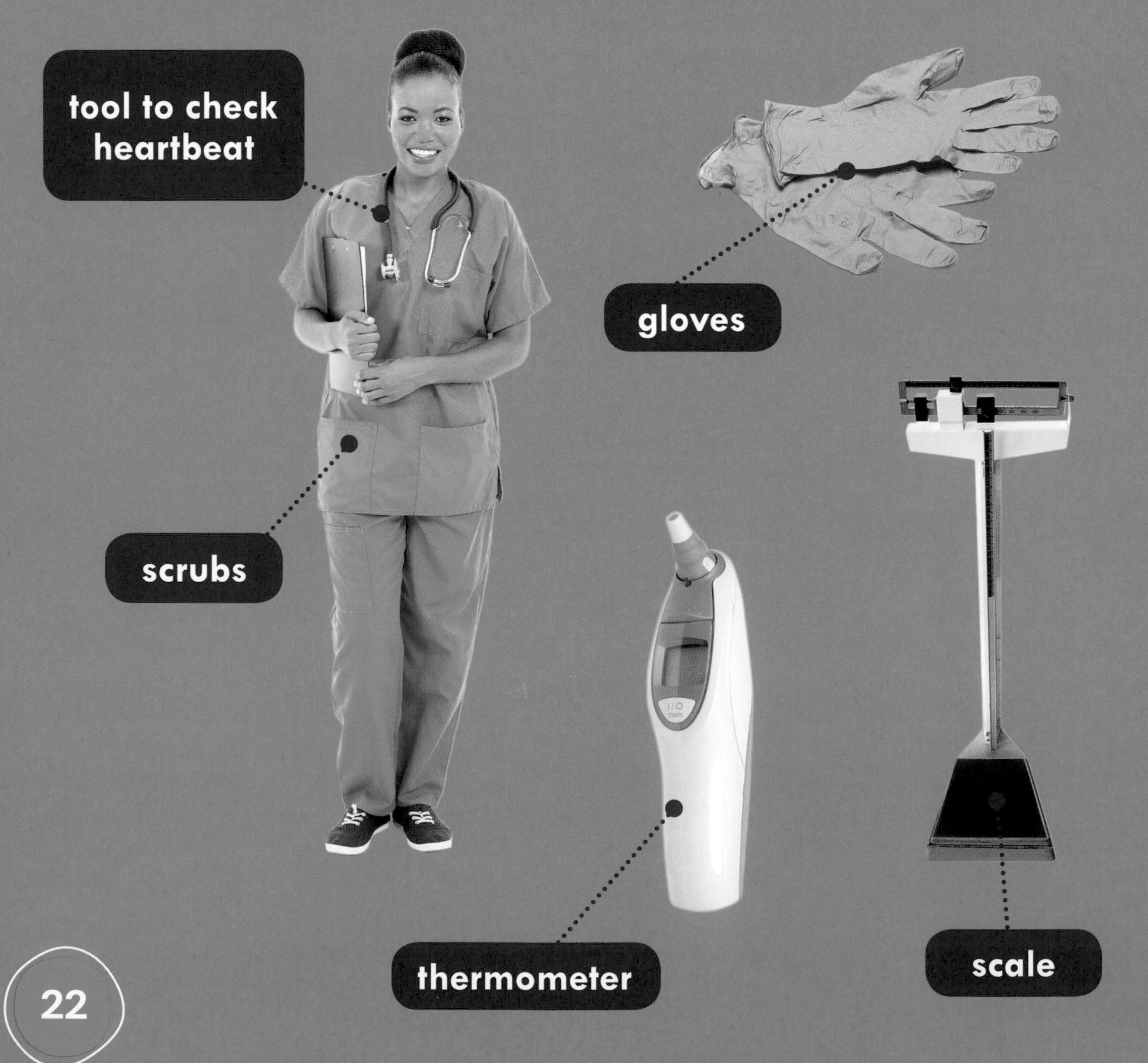
tool to check heartbeat
gloves
scrubs
I/O
mem
thermometer
scale

Picture Glossary

patients

sick or hurt people treated by nurses and doctors

scale

a device that weighs things

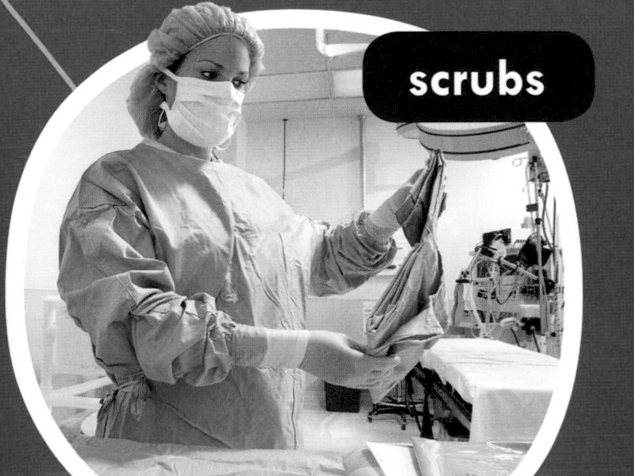

scrubs

uniforms nurses wear

shot

medicine pushed through a needle

Index

Read More

Garrett, Winston. *What Does the School Nurse Do?* New York: PowerKids Press, 2015.

Meister, Cari. *Nurses.* Minneapolis: Bullfrog Books, 2015.

Minden, Cecilia. *Nurses.* Mankato, MN: The Child's World, 2014.

Photo Credits

The images in this book are used with the permission of: © Steve Debenport/iStock.com, pp. 5, 18–19; © Monkey Business Images/Shutterstock.com, pp. 6–7, 20, 23 (top left); © Tyler Olson/Shutterstock.com, p. 9; © Brian Eichhorn/Shutterstock.com, pp. 10–11; © bikeriderlondon/Shutterstock.com, pp. 12, 15, 23 (top right), 23 (bottom left); © Duplass/Shutterstock.com, pp. 16, 23 (bottom right); © michaeljung/Shutterstock.com, p. 22 (left); © Burlingham/Shutterstock.com, p. 22 (top right); © luk/Shutterstock.com, p. 22 (bottom middle); © Brocreative/Shutterstock.com, p. 22 (bottom right).

Front Cover: © michaeljung/iStock.com/Thinkstock.